NICOTEXT

CONFESSIONS

Fredrik Colting
Carl-Johan Gadd
Edited by: Lara Allen

www.nicotext.com
info@nicotext.com

Printed by WS Bookwell, Finland, 2005

ISBN 91-974882-8-3

PREFACE

FORGIVE ME FATHER FOR I HAVE SINNED...
THE PURPOSE OF THIS BOOK IS NOT TO REVEL IN THE MISERY OF OTHERS,
OUR HOPE IS THAT READING IT WILL MAKE YOU FEEL COMPLETELY
"NORMAL". WHEN YOU READ WHAT OTHER ORDINARY PEOPLE HAVE
CONFESSED, IT WILL GIVE YOU PERSPECTIVE ON THE SECRETS YOU
YOURSELF CARRY AROUND.
IT WILL SIMPLY MAKE YOU FEEL LESS LIKE THE ONLY FREAK AROUND.
SECRETS ARE LIKE A BAG OF STONES – IT WILL ONLY GET HEAVIER TO
CARRY OVER TIME.
TO TELL THEIR INNERMOST SECRETS IS A RELIEF TO MANY PEOPLE AND
THE FACT THAT IT'S FUN TO READ WHAT OTHERS HAVE CONFESSED
ONLY MAKES IT BETTER!

UNBURDEN YOUR HEART!

IT WON'T CHANGE ANYTHING, BUT YOU WILL FEEL BETTER!

*THIS BOOK IS A COMPILATION OF ANONYMOUS EMAIL INTERVIEWS.
WE DID NOT TAP THE CONFESSION BOOTH... OR DID WE?

INDEX

KEY TO HELL RATINGS:

 - Slap on the wrist from St. Peter.

 - Two or three Hail Mary's and you're good to go.

 - So this is Purgatory..

 - It's getting hot in here..

 - Burn, baby, Burn!!!

envy

I like this guy, but he already has a girlfriend. I almost hooked up with him before, but since we live so far apart this slut beat me to it. I hate her. I feel like tying her to a chair and paying some guys to pee on her. But I'm ashamed of my feelings.

- Louise, Kindergarten teacher

Hell rating: 🔥🔥🔥

I traded my Cindy doll's lovely ballerina skirt for an ugly blue and white sailor dress when I was eight. I still regret it. It's twenty one years ago. I've resented the girl I traded with ever since and wouldn't mind hitting her over the head.

- "Anonymous in Anger", 28

Hell rating:

I'm secretly a transvestite and get off on wearing women's clothing.
The more formal the outfit, the more turned on I get.
I've ordered several wedding dresses online. When they get here I'll put
on panties, bra, pantyhose, gloves, underskirt, dress – everything –
and lie on my bed and jerk off.

I'm also turned on by wearing diapers.

- Vincent, 43

Hell Rating:

I found my ex-boyfriend's condoms at a party at his and his new girlfriend's house. I poked a needle through all of the condoms.

Hope the girlfriend gets pregnant!

- Erika, 20

Hell Rating: 🔥🔥🔥🔥🔥

I hereby confess to trying to find my best friend's wife's panties whenever I visit their home. I can't resist the temptation of holding them, caressing them, and smelling her on them.
I'm very worried that that they'll catch me, but can't suppress my desire for the forbidden fruit. I really like my best friend, and would never wish him any harm.

I want just his wife's knickers.

- Samuel, 39, Self-employed

Hell Rating:

I'm disgustingly fake. Officially, I'm against racism, but I think racist thoughts every day. I like gay men if anyone asks, but am secretly very much against them. I dislike the upper class with their servants but my highest wish is to have a cleaning lady. I think that old people smell bad. I want to have sex with pretty much every guy I meet while everyone I know thinks that I'd never even think like that.
I have many lesbian friends but I honestly think that they're only gay because it's trendy. I'm incredibly fake.

- "Secretly a Sham", 26

Hell Rating:

I sometimes feel it would be nice if someone close to me died so that I could have a good cry. Fairly selfish, but then I could be comforted and then have sex with the person who comforted you.

I once pretended to be disabled just so that an old couple would help me open my door.

- "Anonymous Affection-Seeker", 36

Hell Rating:

When I went to the swimming pool a few days ago, I found bottles of brand new shampoo and conditioner (one of those expensive hair salon brands) that someone had "forgotten". I quickly put them in my backpack. When I returned from swimming, a woman asked me if I had seen anyone take her bottles. I said no. I don't think she believed me, but I don't give a damn! Now I'll have nice hair!

 I also peed in the pool just before getting out.

- "Unknown Shampoo Usurper", 34

Hell Rating:

I use my binoculars to watch people in the apartments across the street. You wouldn't believe me if I told you all the things people do when they think noone is watching.

This is a dirty little habit of mine, but I can't stop.

- Carl, 46, on disability pension

Hell Rating: 🔥🔥

I like the atmosphere every time there's a catastrophe like the September 11th thing. I enjoy all the activities surrounding it and you always have something to talk about with everyone you meet.

I know it's sick.

- Lara, 46

Hell Rating: 🔥🔥🔥🔥🔥

I get jealous when my girlfriend goes clubbing.
But I know that she'd never cheat. Ever. Or would she?

- "Anonymous Agonizer", 23

Hell Rating: 🔥 🔥

I usually steal my friends' stories, but with myself as the main character. In my real life nothing ever happens.

- Edgar, Accountant, 42

Hell Rating:

I go around town with a crutch sometimes just to see peoples reactions. If you fall or drop the crutch when you are getting up from a bench, most people just walk by.

I really like it when people feel sorry for me.

- Julia, 38, Secretary

Hell Rating:

sloth

I pee in the shower but will never admit it to anyone.
I think I'm with my boyfriend because I don't want to
lose a place to sleep.

- Linda

Hell Rating:

Once, at a house warming party at a friend's house, I went to do
"number two". After squeezing out a huge one, there was no toilet
paper. so I used his bathrobe to dry myself. Sorry buddy, it was me!

- "The Unnamed Bum Wiper", 18

Hell Rating:

I'm supposed to work forty hours a week. I never work that much.
I'm always coming in late in the morning and leaving early in the
afternoon. During the day, I do the bare minimum: nothing more.
I'm so tired, I can't get out of bed in the morning. I'm arriving at work
later and later. One day, I fell asleep on my chair in the office.
Luckily, the phone rang before I fell off my chair.
I just want to sleep.

- "Anonymous Analyst", 38

Hell Rating:

I throw old food on my neighbour's lawn because I'm too lazy to go all the way to the trash can and throw it away myself. I've been doing it for more than two years now.

It amuses me greatly when he finds the leftover food. Hahaha

- "Top-Secret Trash Tosser", 27

Hell Rating:

I bumped into a car while parking my car earlier. It got a substantial dent on its rear bumper, but my car didn't get a mark on it.
I drove away without saying a thing.

- "Stealthy Smasher", 30

Hell Rating:

I eat my own snot.

- Fredrik, 28, Self-employed

Hell Rating:

For two years, I told my girlfriend every night that I loved her when I felt nothing for her. Then I got the guts to break up.

My only regret is that I didn't do it sooner.

- "Delayed Dumper", 36

Hell Rating:

At every job I've had, I've avoided actually working. My exterior-the way I carry myself-gives the impression that I'm very dependable, and they've all believed my lies.
Once a co-worker out buying lunch caught me out on the town when I should have been working. Since I wasn't fired, I guess she didn't tell anyone.
I put in a maximum of four hours of work per eight-hour day.

- "Sluggish Salesman" , 34

Hell Rating:

When I shave "down there" I use my dad's shaver...
needless to say he doesn't know about it.

- "Secret Shaver", 17, Student

Hell Rating:

I'm a bad person. I don't recycle, I'm lazy at work, I have two lovers who don't know that the other one exists, I fart on the couch, pee in the shower and everyone thinks I'm this bloody perfect, sweet and well-mannered young woman. I'm not one bit ashamed!!

- Sofie, 28, Shop assistant

Hell Rating:

Once, when I was at the movies, I had to pee real bad. I ran out of the theatre looking for the toilets, but, to my horror, I couldn't find them. As a last resort, I went behind a screen in a corner where they stored some cleaning equipment.
There I was, on the nice red carpet – peeing.

- Mia, 28, Assistant editor

Hell Rating:

A year ago, I was crossing the street. An elderly woman was lying face down in the snow. I passed her by without doing a thing.

I still feel terrible.

- Elisabeth, Principal

Hell Rating:

My neighbour was stuck in the elevator today, she called out when I passed by but I pretended not to hear.

Sorry, neighbour.

- "Nasty Neighbor", 50

Hell Rating: 🔥🔥🔥

When I worked at a paint store, I knowingly sold varnish designed for industrial concrete floors to the owner of a newly built house with parquet flooring.

The floor was completely corroded and destroyed.

- "Poor-grade Paint Hawker", 25

Hell Rating: 🔥 🔥 🔥

I poured a small amount of alcohol, about a cap, in my girlfriend's friend's aquarium at a party once.
 All the fish died.

I never told anyone.

- Libby, 34, Artist

Hell Rating:

I blow my nose on people, but not so they notice.
A morning hobby I fear has gone too far.

- Eric, Hospital Orderly

Hell Rating:

I blow my nose on the toilet paper before wiping my ass with it. It's a bit yucky, but if anyone caught me doing it I'd just say that it's better than doing it the other way around.

- "Hush-Hush Hornblower", 38

Hell Rating:

More often than not, I'm so lazy I'll grab a cab to go to a place that's a ten-minute walk away. If I'm going there to meet a friend, I simply get out of the cab around the corner from the meeting place.
My friends think I walk everywhere. I feel awfully guilty about this, but find it hard to break this habitual laziness.

- Cathy, Illustrator

Hell Rating:

I´m really sick of work, so a while ago I simply stopped answering my emails. I know that many people have tried to email me, wanting stuff from me, and when they call I say that there must be something wrong with their email. It´s worked for 4 weeks now.

- Matthew, 29, Customer service

Hell Rating:

I never wash after I´ve been to the toilet. I do put the water on though, just to make it sound as if I do wash my hands.

- Suzanna, 26, Waitress

Hell Rating:

gluttony

I worked as a cleaner in a store a few years back, working the floor polisher early in the morning before the staff arrived. I noticed that they were having a competition; you had to guess the weight of a giant (foam-rubber) cookie. I made sure the coast was clear, took the giant cookie to a scale, and weighed it. I wrote the answer on a note and put it in the box. Guess who won her weight in cookies?

- "Cookie Monster", Maid, 33

Hell Rating:

Oh, no! I did it again. I can't not do it. I was at a friend's flat today and when she had to go to the loo, I jumped at the opportunity to read her diary. I've read a lot from it and know just about everything about her and her boyfriend. I know that she's cheated on him and more dirt like that.

It feels fucking great to read other people's diaries.

Do it!

- Jenny, 22, Student

Hell Rating:

When I baby sit little kids, I leave them alone to make them scared and sad. I do this so I can comfort them. It's such a great feeling when they desperately throw themselves in my arms. Later I feel a bit bad about being so mean to them.

But I can't help it.

- Tanya, Child Care

Hell Rating:

These days when I shop for pick-n-mix candy, I weigh the bag after a while, keep the price tag and keep on picking more candy. When I've got what I want, I close the bag with the price tag I took earlier. I always shop for candy this way. No regrets here.

It's so expensive these days.

- Margret, 69, Senior Citizen

Hell Rating: 🔥🔥🔥

I take the fat off the ham and the pork chops at home and feed it to our poodle, Fifi, when no one sees me. Now our dog is getting fat as a pig and by parents don't understand why.
So they're mad at Fifi. Sorry, Fifi, and sorry Mom and Dad.

- "Pigging out the Poodle", 19

Hell Rating:

I work in health care and chew pain killers and sedatives every day at work. Free access. I keep appearances up, though, and am no stranger to complaining if a colleague has been out the night before and smells like it at work. When I worked with the ambulance crew, my colleague and I got high on nitrous oxide and partied all night. One of the other employees got blamed for the high consumption of nitrous oxide.

- Anonymous Ambulance Worker, 34

Hell Rating:

I can't stop squeezing the cream filled pastries when I'm at the supermarket. It's like some kind of reversed phobia.

- Tim, 26, Advertising

Hell Rating:

I collect paper of the right "stiffness". Not as thin as newspapers,
but not as thick as the cover of magazines. Something in the middle is
best. The surface has to be matt, not glossy, or it will tear too easily.
With it I do this:
I cut them in pieces, 1? x 1? inches and pile them.
Later, when I'm watching movies, TV or surfing the net, I fold the paper
into different shapes and feel its texture. Good paper is a real pleasure
and I always take a bunch whenever I find good quality flyers.
The sweetest thing my (fantastic) girlfriend ever did for me was to
remember what kind of paper I prefer and go to the library to get
me some.

True love.

- Andy, 29

Hell Rating: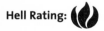

pride

I'm gay but live in a straight relationship which I don't have the guts to end.

- Martin, Receptionist

Hell Rating: 🔥🔥🔥

I'm too afraid to confess to my mom that I'm seeing a man forty years my senior.

I don't know what to do.

- Ramona, 22

Hell Rating: 🔥🔥

I committed a crime an innocent person was blamed for.
Two months later, that person died in a car crash and everyone
was said "only goes to prove - you get what you deserve".

I feel bad because of this.

- Anonymous in Agony, 29

Hell Rating:

I erased my best friend's big university essay two days before it was due.

He thinks it was a virus.

Sorry.

- Anonymous Good Buddy, 23

Hell Rating:

I'm 42 years old and a virgin.

- "Unused", 42

Hell Rating:

I'm a man and I wear a wig every day.
No one at work knows this.
I used to have long hair when I was younger, but over the years, my hair line has been receding and the hair is getting thinner.
Tried wearing a wig for fun one time and it went well.
Sometimes people even compliment me on my long hair.

I graciously accept.

- "Wacky Wigger", 32, Bank Employee

Hell Rating: 🔥 🔥

I tell my girlfriend that I think her food tastes great, but it really tastes like rubber.

I'd rather eat disgusting food than see her sad.

- Peter, Musician

Hell Rating:

I'm a Muslim but I don't wear a veil. I've moved out of my parents' house and when I'm with my friends I talk about sex with them. Sometimes when I'm with them, I even eat hot dogs.
My parents don't know. My brother knows, but he does the same thing so it doesn't matter.

- "Mysterious Muslim", 21, Student

Hell Rating:

I'm not sure I love my children equally. I'm not even sure I love them more than anything. I sometimes dream about running away to get a fresh start.

Without children.

- "Furtive Father" , 40, Sales Rep.

Hell Rating:

When I was out driving my car, the elderly lady in the car in front of me stopped much sooner than needed at a traffic light. To get back at her, I honked my horn before the light had changed back to green. The lady drove into oncoming traffic and was hit. Her car was completely trashed, though nobody was hurt. I told the police I had accidentally hit the horn while looking for a CD on the floor.

Sorry, lady.

Your nice Peugeot was bent like a cheese doodle.

- "Anonymous Auto Trasher", 27

Hell Rating:

I like to smell my own farts.

- Andrew, Marketing Director

Hell Rating:

I'm a vegetarian, but I eat meat when no one sees. So I'm not really a vegetarian. I don't know why I do this, why I try to keep up appearances. None of my friends are vegetarians, so I have no "peer pressure" forcing me to continue. Maybe I want to be a vegetarian, but am failing.

- "Anonymous Meat Eater", 26

Hell Rating:

I have unwillingly taken a shit in my pants at three different occasions as an adult.
I'd never tell anyone about this;

it's far to embarrassing.

- "Beleagured about Bowels", 40, Interpreter

Hell Rating:

I always try to give people around me as bad a conscience as possible. I tell my mom that my dad hurts me, my boyfriend that he always does and says things that hurt my feelings. To my friends I say I'm depressed and feel bad. I only do these things to get attention and hugs and things like that. In reality I feel great and even more so when I'm in the centre of attention.

- "Anonymous Attention Hog", 21

Hell Rating:

I got an A+ on my special project in high school but I didn't do it myself. I found it on the internet. It got a bit tricky when the teacher asked me to give an oral presentation when I hadn't even read it.

- "Covert Cheater", 22,

Hell Rating: 🔥 🔥 🔥 🔥 🔥

I have a passion for peeing everywhere but in the toilet, but only in public restrooms. Usually, I pee in the sink and on the faucet. At my university, I pee in the wastebasket in the bathroom. Once, at IKEA, there was no sink in the bathroom so I tried to fill the toilet brush holder instead. I peed all over the floor.

Perhaps I'm sick?

- David, 27, Student

Hell Rating:

I'm a 28-year-old guy, but everyone around me thinks I'm 21. I really don't want to lie any more; I want everyone to know my real age.

There. Now I feel better.

- "Lying Liar", 28

Hell Rating: 🔥🔥

I'm sitting here with a university bachelor's degree in media and communication – and I have cheated my way through my entire education. My entire essay was made up in one week and is all a lie – made up studies and other nonsense.

- "Storytelling Student", 22

Hell Rating: 🔥🔥🔥

Sometimes when I'm peeing in a public bathroom I back away from the toilet towards the door to test my long distance peeing skills.

- Mike, 38, Accountant

Hell Rating:

Some years ago, I went to a party at the county governor's residence. One of the rooms there serves as home away from home for some senator.

My friend and I rubbed our dicks on his pillow.

- Martin, Military

Hell Rating:

I have tons of books, but haven't read them all. I sometimes say I have.

- Carl, Publisher

Hell Rating:

Once, I backed into a brand new Volvo with my car— a piece of crap compared to the Volvo. I made a huge dent in the Volvo's door. Lying comes easily to me, if it makes me look better.

- Nina, 30, Librarian

Hell Rating:

I'm the son of one of the most written about managing directors in the country. I have a huge apartment and lead a luxurious life in the inner circle of high society. Officially, I listen to U2, Beatles and Elvis and stuff. But when I'm alone. I listen to music like Cypress Hill and dream of living like an average Joe. I get lots of girls who want nothing more then to get their hands on my family money. I buy them what ever they want, just to get them in bed - and I get them there. I do cocaine on the weekend because it's better and basically free for us.

I hate my life, to be honest and myself.

- "Spoiled Sponge", 25

Hell Rating:

I'm a left-wing activist and say that I hate the upper class, but at the same time. I'm of noble birth and have tens of thousands in the bank.

- Lydia, 39

Hell Rating:

I went skiing with my boyfriend one week last winter and I didn't go "number two" all week. I was afraid he'd smell it, hear it or see skid marks.

- "Anonymous and Anal Retentive"

Hell Rating:

I managed to get into Mensa by cheating on the IQ-test! I "borrowed" a book with the test from a friend, a Mensa member, a few days before the test. Some friends and I spent a few days figuring out the answers. Since there were no answers in the book, we had to put some effort into it. But all went well and now I'm a member! I'd never have passed the test without all the extra time and help from my friends.

- "Deceiving Genius", 28

Hell Rating: 🔥 🔥 🔥

I'm actually quite rich, but pretend to be like everyone else - a poor student. It's rather fun to play poor and pretend to have to "turn every penny". Mean as I am, I enjoy calling in petty cash loans from friends, even though the money means nothing to me and a hell of a lot more to them.

- Simon, 26, student

Hell Rating:

I think that my sister's kids are the UGLIEST kids in the world.
She thinks that they are totally cute and I lie and say that they are cute.
Oh my lord! She's my own sister after all.

- "Adoring Auntie", 30

Hell Rating:

I made a list of everyone, EVERYONE, I had had sex with and added comments after the names. When I started dating my boyfriend, I hid the list in a really clever place in the apartment among some equipment for a freezer I don't use. The thing is, that I've had sex with more than 60 guys and really didn't want my boyfriend to find the list. It's just that the hiding place was so good, that I forgot to take the list with me when I moved, and the people who took over the apartment are coworkers of mine.

Oddly enough, they have stopped saying 'hello' to me.

- Anonymous Adlibber

Hell Rating:

I've never cheated on anyone, but I say that I have. No one would believe me if I told the truth since I sleep around quite a bit when I'm single.

I am now considering having an affair to make my lies true.

- Anonymous in Adultery

Hell Rating: ( ) ( ) ( )

I always pee in the water when I swim in a public pool.

- Krystle, 42, Psychologist

Hell Rating: 🔥🔥

I'm a mythomaniac. I even told my best friends that I'm getting treatment for this

but I'm not.

- Marie the Storyteller

Hell Rating: 🔥🔥🔥

I secretly find my boyfriend to be an idiot. I tell my mom this when I talk to her on the phone.

I'm with him because he pays for my internet access.

- Eleonora

Hell Rating:

I'm petrified that I'll shit myself.
I feel socially crippled.

- Tony, Marketing

Hell Rating:

I'm gay but I've never told anyone.
Not even my wife.

- Man, 42

Hell Rating:

I'm a pilot working for a major airline and I hate my job. I actually find it very unpleasant to fly; you might even say I have a fear of flying. It's mainly during take-off and landing. The only reason I'm a pilot is because it was expected of me - both my dad and granddad were pilots. This is completely stressing me out and all I can think about is how to get out of this with my honour intact.

- Petrified Pilot, 32

Hell Rating:

I find sex to be quite boring actually.
Like some kind of bad gymnastics.

But when I talk about sex I make it sound like I love it.

- "Tedious Tenderness", 36

Hell Rating:

Sometimes I pretend to cry in front of my boyfriend because I want him to feel sorry for me and because I want the attention.

- "Watch Me Weep", 19

Hell Rating:

I always wash my hands after I've taken a shower.
Just to be safe, you know.

This can't be good.

- Mike, 33

Hell Rating:

I'm a professed Christian, but I regularly masturbate to porn I've downloaded off the internet. I've lived a very calm life, but have everyone convinced that I'm a real bad seed.

I'm a big coward.

- Pamela, 32

Hell Rating:

I bought a $9000 motorbike. I've driven it about thirty miles and feel scared the whole time. The only reason I bought it was so that I could say that "I drive a heavy motorbike". I hang in this bikers' forum on the net where they think I'm this hard guy who really can drive – to them I'm a bit of a legend. If they only knew that I sometimes almost cry when I accidentally give more gas I'm so scared.
It's a pain.

Soon I'll sell it and claim I had a bad fall.

- Jimmy, 39, CEO

Hell Rating:

To everyone's knowledge I'm a vegetarian,
but I eat hamburgers when no one can see me.

- Alexandra, Student

Hell Rating:

I can't afford a TV, so when my friends talk about shows they've
seen the day before, I pretend to have seen them, too.

I can't admit that I don't have a TV.

- Li, Shop Assistant

Hell Rating:

I have a disgusting habit. When I´m in bed and I fart, I pull the covers over my head and smell my own gas.

- Aaron, Security Guard, 24

Hell Rating:

When me and my girlfriend have had sex I always get really unsure if she had an orgasm or not. It´s gone so far now that everytime we have sex I keep her under close inspection to see if she´s faking it.

I wish I was a girl.

- Simon, Teacher, 33

Hell Rating:

Sometimes when my wife is away on business I still order two pizzas or buy two steaks at the foodstore. I don´t want people to think, "poor, lonely guy. Why is he single? What´s wrong with him?"

- Pat, 40, Writer

Hell Rating:

I cried when I saw the movie "Finding Nemo", the part when Nemo discovered he didn´t have as nice a fin as the other fishes.
I mean I´m a man and I cry over a cartoon fish!

- Andy, 38, Fireman

Hell Rating:

greed

I travelled around Thailand for 6 months, enjoying it immensely... even more so every other Thursday when the money from the unemployment benefit found arrived in my account.

- "Jobless Jaunter", 31

Hell Rating: 🔥🔥🔥

A few years back, we had a substitute mailman where I lived.
One day I got a letter in my mail slot that should have gone to my
neighbour two stories up. It was a standard white envelope.
When I held it up to the light I saw that it contained a bill.
It was $50... which I kept.

- "Good Neighbour-Guy", 48

Hell Rating:

Yesterday I stole a WLAN-router/hub, worth g180 (about $230).
I just hooked it up. Now I'm having a wonderful time!
It was so easy, and I'm worth it. It makes me feel great to have wireless
access to the net from more than up to 253 computers at the same time.

- Jerry, 30, Systems Engineer

Hell Rating:

I listen in on my neighbours' phone calls.

- "Erstwhile Eavesdropper", 32, Sales

Hell Rating:

When I'm in someone's home, regardless if it's a friend, family or strangers, I take scissors and cut off some of my pubic hair and hide it in a weird place in the house. I don't know why I do it, but I can't stop.

- Frida, Artist

Hell Rating:

I never pay full price on the train.
I always buy a ticket to go one or two stations, and then I travel all over on the same train. It's that easy.

I plan to poison the idiots at work by putting something in the coffee vending-machine, perhaps.

- Elisabeth, 43, Interior decorator

Hell Rating:

I've promised to move in with my ex to get access to fast internet broad-band, but she thinks I love her and want to get back together.

- Paul, 24, Student

Hell Rating:

I worked for a big company for three years. During this time, I swindled at least $30.000 out of the company. I got caught... but was only busted for $500 and that's all I have to reimburse. No regrets whatsoever.

- David, 47, Unemployed

Hell Rating: 🔥🔥🔥

I sell information about the company I work for to an old high school friend's dad.

- Charlie, 29

Hell Rating: 🔥🔥🔥

I sat next to a man on the subway this morning. When he got up to leave a hundred dollar bill fell out of his pocket. It landed behind my bag. I didn't say anything and he left. I spent the money on a DVD player. Sorry, Gramps.

I ran over an unfortunate rabbit with my car on my way home from work last week.

- John, 43, Cab driver

Hell Rating: 🔥🔥🔥🔥

I borrow my old grandmother's parking permit and park for free downtown.

- Lisa, 29, Web designer

Hell Rating:

A co-worker and I were drinking wine at my place. When she was leaving, I followed her out to her bike. When I leaned on the door of a shop it opened; it wasn't locked. This was at midnight, so of course we were the only ones there. We entered the empty store. We took all the food we could carry and the cash from the open register. There was almost $1400. She took every cigarette pack—fifteen grocery bags in total— some food vouchers and 200 lottery tickets which gave us $1000 more. I feel bad about this. I'm 29 and the mother of two children. I've never stolen before.

- "Purloining Parent", 29

Hell Rating: 🔥🔥🔥🔥

When I was a child I'd steal apples from an old lady's back garden, walk to her front door, ring it, and give her the apples. I thought I was being very nice to her. One time we broke her mailbox. I regret this.

She is dead now.

- Charlotte, Nurse

Hell Rating:

I'm your average reliable bloke... or so everyone thinks. I spend much of my time thinking about "becoming a criminal". The thought of stealing now consumes almost all of my waking hours.

- "Fanciful Felon", 42

Hell Rating:

When I was at Bloomingdale's today I found a mobile phone on one of the half price tables. I turned it off and put it in my bag. I'm now the very-pleased owner of a brand new Nokia that I got for free!

Does this constitute as stealing?

- Cindy, 18

Hell Rating:

I once found a wallet at one of the hippest clubs in Miami. In it were a few hundred bucks and a bank card with its code. I spent the money and withdrew a couple of hundred more from the account.

The next day, I called the owner of the wallet to inform her that I'd found her wallet – empty, unfortunately. Two days later, we met, I returned the wallet, and let her buy me a delicious dinner as a token of her appreciation. I was going to screw her too, but she was too hideous. I'm just too awful.

- "Deceiving Dining Companion", 24

Hell Rating:

Once, when I was young and stupid, I went with an old man into a toilet and showed him my boobs. I got $20.

To this day I still don't understand why.

- Tina, 42, nurse

Hell Rating:

When I was a kid, I found a frog in the woods. When my family was going home again, I politely asked my mom if I could keep the frog and bring it home with us but she said no. She said that the frog belonged in the woods, but the frog was so cute that I decided to ignore her and bring it anyway. I smuggled it into the car. The car was boiling hot and my hands very warm. I remember holding the frog in my left hand. It probably died from being over heated or suffocation. When we got home and I checked on it it didn't move. I have killed an innocent frog. I'm ashamed.

- "Frog-Killer", 30

Hell Rating:

My former boyfriend and I arranged a small insurance fraud by saying that he'd had $250 in rent money in his wallet and a pair of slalom skis when he got robbed. We collected $450 and went on vacation.
We had a receipt for the skis and a withdrawal slip from the bank, but we still had both the money and the skis.

- Kirsten, 42, Designer

Hell Rating:

I'm a police officer with a bad habit. I shoplift whenever I enter a store. It makes me feel very guilty, but no one checks my uniform pockets.

- Richard, Police officer

Hell Rating:

I tend to steal things in town on my way home. One shovel and one house number sign. Number 28. If you need a sign like that, feel free to contact me! The TV-subscription might be worth mentioning; I don't even know who to pay it to.

- "Compulsive Creeper", 33

Hell Rating:

I saw someone drop his wallet. My buddy and I discreetly "stole" the wallet and grabbed the cash. The next day I called the owner and told him that I'd found his wallet. He was really happy and gave me a reward - £30 (about $55). I should feel bad about this, but I don't. Maybe I feel a bit ashamed.

I'm sorry, God.

- Sandy, Student

Hell Rating:

The only reason I'm with my boyfriend is that he's rich.

- "Loyal Lover", 26

Hell Rating:

I've had a television ever since I moved out of my parents' house a few years back, but I've never paid for my cable.

I'm sorry.

- Carly, 27, Producer

Hell Rating:

I worked at an amusement park this summer where a visitor gave me a digital camera that someone had lost. I never bothered to look for the real owner. Instead, I sold the camera to a friend of mine for fifty bucks. Another time a man brought in a wallet. I looked at the picture on the driving license and realized that the owner had just been in and I ran out to give it back to him. Ha was so happy! He was pushing his disabled wife around in a wheelchair and he was a bit on the slow side himself.

I guess these two events sort of even each other out.

- "Tit for Tat", 20

Hell Rating:

I've been working while being on disability pension. It will cost me a lot if they catch me. I don't feel one bit ashamed, even though I know what I'm doing is very wrong. I just pretend to be a mental case.
I'm completely healthy, and enjoy leading a comfortable life.

- Harley, 40

Hell Rating:

One summer while working for the Catholic Church, I was in charge of the mail service. They had one of these stamp machines that you pre-load with money, kind of like a credit card. Before I understood that, I printed a stamp worth $9999, just for the fun of it.

They never found out.

- "Steep Stamping", 24, Student

Hell Rating:

I lied about having an abortion to get money from a guy. Even though we'd used a condom, I told him he'd have to pay for my suffering. A hundred bucks, which I spent on clothes.

- "Lying Mother", 19

Hell Rating:

If I could choose between my grandmother dying or me getting $ 10.000, I would choose the money.

- Lisa, 40, nurse

Hell Rating:

When I´m drunk and walking home from the bar I keep my eyes open for Mercedes cars. If I find one I snatch the hood ornament. I have 19 of them in my closet but I dont know what to do with them.

E-bay maybe?

- Paul, 22, Bartender

Hell Rating:

urath

Every time I see a small dog,
I want to place my foot under its belly and lob it into the air.

They seem to be made for it.

One fine day I'll do it.

- Anonymous Dog Lover

Hell Rating:

I used my position as a teacher at a high school to enter the school archives and gather information on former students who were Nazis. I gave the information to friends of mine who used it to destroy the lives of these students.

- Anonymous, 35, Teacher

Hell Rating:

I hate it when people insist on telling me about their problems.
But I pretend to listen.

- Michelle. 33, Telephone operator

Hell Rating:

I scolded one of the junior judges during a sports tournament where I coached a mixed team with boys and girls aged 10 – 12. I later found out that some of the judges gave up on judging after that. I'm very sorry, but in my defense I have to say that he had the worst feel for the game I'd ever seen. I'm sorry. I hope you keep judging. I mean it.

- Tom, 46, Systems Operator

Hell Rating:

I work at a nursing home and I play with the notion of mercy killing the sickest patients.

- Stewart, 29

Hell Rating:

I went down to a local construction site one night and moved around some of their markers... a few yards here and there. The next day they dug up a telephone line and a heating power line.

- Marty, Student

Hell Rating:

Right after my parents' divorce, I found out my dad had a new girlfriend. I was feeling very bad at the time and so I cut school to go to his place. I found the new girlfriend's toothbrush. I immediately knew what to do. First I peed and then I cleaned the toilet with the toothbrush before returning it to where I'd found it. I didn't feel bad at all at the time, but now that I've gotten to know her, and know that she's a nice person, I do feel a bit bad about what I did.
But I did get praise from my mom for my little "feat"!

- Melany, 24, Waitress

Hell Rating: 🔥 🔥 🔥 🔥

When I was a kid, I was bullied the entire time I went to school. I was a tiny, skinny, totally weak boy with a torrent of words that could drive anyone insane. One day, after lunch, I stood outside the cafeteria waiting for a boy from first grade. When he was leaving the cafeteria, I pulled open the door as far as I could before letting it swing back (it was a swing door) and hit him in the head. He was in a lot of pain, bleeding and crying. This was misdirected revenge from my side. I was just too afraid to go after any of my real tormentors and instead I made this little innocent boy suffer.

If you read this, please forgive me!

- "Angry Avenger", 39

Hell Rating:

I use tobacco even though I'm underage. I'm also forbidden to do it by my parents, but I do it anyway.
Sometimes I make jokes about mentally retarded people just because my friends do it. I'm ashamed. Forgive me.

- "Secret and Sensitive", 15

Hell Rating: 🔥🔥🔥

When I ride the bus, I always sit in the back and press the stop button before every stop. Being in my sixties, I never worry that anyone will suspect me. I always give the nearest young person a stern look.

- George, 63, Senior Citizen

Hell Rating: 🔥 🔥 🔥

This summer, I gave a blind man a slap across the face when he accidentally bumped into me. He screamed in horror. It was a stupid thing to do and I'm very much ashamed.

- Tina, 36, Mother

Hell Rating:

Once, when I was home alone, I took my family's two mice and gave them to our cat. I wanted to know what it would look like. I regret it. I don't understand why I did it. I'm a vegetarian, after all. I just had to do it... I'm sorry, mice! I love you!

- Danielle, 20, Unemployed

Hell Rating:

I'm over thirty and for the last ten years I've called people up on the phone and farted them in the ear before hanging up on them.

- "Gaseous" , 35, Restaurant Manager

Hell Rating:

I hated my ex so much that I figured out an easy way to kill him. I peed and spat in his vitamin drink, rubbed his toothbrush on my anus, and peed on his gum shield (he's a hockey player). The worst part is that I enjoyed it when he drank his vitamin drink. I smiled when he brushed his teeth. I can tell you that he did NOT know how to treat a girlfriend. He's currently serving in the UN and I hope he steps on a mine.

- Mia, Aerobics Instructor

Hell Rating:

A friend and I turned a speed limit sign once. On one side, it said 50 and on the other 20 m.p.h. We only flipped it 180 degrees so that the nice and flat road got the 20 m.p.h speed limit and the road with speed bumps on it got 50! I hope no one got hurt.

- Mike, Student

Hell Rating:

The tree that lit up my family's dark winter days and nights during Christmas was stolen.
Necessity knows no law.

- Joey, Insurance Broker

Hell Rating:

Once I was so bloody tired of my budgies (birds) that I opened my kitchen window and let them out into the freezing winter weather. They flew away. I suppose that they froze to death later.
If you can hear me now, I'm sorry.

- Margot, 29, Store Manager

Hell Rating:

I once ran over a cat with my car. Since it didn't stop moving, I backed over it. When I was done it was completely flat. An old lady watched me. Perhaps it was her cat.

- Fredrik, 46, Restaurant Owner

Hell Rating:

I have a hard time keeping my emotions in check when I drive. I curse and scream and call other drivers bad names. There have been times when I've wanted to step out of my car and kill people, hit them over the head with an iron pipe so that their head cracks open and their brains runs out onto the sidewalk.

- Peter, 32, Lawyer

Hell Rating:

My former boyfriend told me that he wanted to take a shit on me so I dumped him.
No one would believe this if I told them.

You simply don't think he's that kind of guy.

- Darcy, 35, Sales Rep.

Hell Rating:

I open my window a bit, lie down on the floor. and shout instructions to the people on the street below—like "stop", "look out", "I'll kick your ass you bastard" or general four-letter words.
I've also thrown food at people from my window.

- "Violent Voices" , 44, Public Relations

Hell Rating:

I backed over my brother's-in-law cat with my car. I threw it in a paper recycling dumpster and never told anyone about it.

- "Anonymous Animal Killer", 46

Hell Rating: 🔥 🔥 🔥

I was standing in line today at the store when one guy cuts in front of me, pushing his way to the front of the line. I wanted to kill him; just take his head and bang it against a glass window until he was covered in blood. Then I'd kick him in the stomach until he died.
It's a good thing I'm such a coward.

- Billy, 37, Waiter

Hell Rating:

I sometimes enter a bird forum on the site www.parrot.net and give people anonymous advice so that their birds die or at least get really sick.
I know nothing about birds, but no one there gets that.
If they don't know any better themselves it is probably for the best that their birds die.

- Peter, 39, Hairdresser

Hell Rating:

I hate slow people!
I also hate people who stop and stand in the way.
I hate senior citizens who stand in the way with their two shopping carts waiting for better times.

There are no better times ahead!!!

- Sarah, 32, On maternity leave

Hell Rating:

I lead a very proper life with a great job, salary, benefits and family, but I feel all this stress and pressure. All the demands sometimes makes me feel like I would like to do something completely crazy, like running through the office with a machine gun and shoot everyone here. Just to get them to shut the fuck up and stop putting demands on me.

- Larry, 50, chief of marketing

Hell Rating:

When my managers aren't watching I sometimes spit in their food in the refrigerator. They don't know that I talk trash about them behind their backs or that I watch porn on my computer during office hours.

- "Secret Spitter", 32

Hell Rating:

This completely stuck-up gas station owner really pissed me off. He was rude and cocky. At 6 the next morning, he had fast drying glue and a broken off match in every lock at his gas station. Serves him right. Unfortunately I could not stay and watch him try to open them. He has had his locks glued every time I've been in our nation's capital.

- "Gluing and Gasing", 26

Hell Rating:

Once, I was at a party at this self-absorbed, stupid, pushy and annoying guy's place. Just before leaving, I went to the bathroom. When I was done peeing I discovered that there was no toilet paper, so I dried myself thoroughly on his towel instead. Serves him right for feeling me up when I clearly didn't want him to.

- Marie, 34, Self-employed

Hell Rating:

Sometimes I get to borrow my boss' car.
I drive it in first gear for as long as possible.

- Luke, 29, Sales rep.

Hell Rating:

Last week I got my hands on someone's credit card number online and used it to buy bootleg alcohol to send to the Jehovah's witnesses across the street from me.

- "Thieven' for Jesus", 27

Hell Rating:

Once, when I was really mad at my boyfriend (at the time), I peed on his toothbrush as revenge. I didn't tell him until much later and laughed so hard that he didn't know what to think.
But it was all true. At the time I thought that he deserved it,
but now it seems a bit too much.

- "Tinkle Teeth", 23

Hell Rating:

My friends often come to me for advice. Mainly relationship advice. The problem is, that I don't want to give advice. The worst thing that can happen is that they actually take it. So far, I have managed to arrange one divorce and for two people to quit their jobs. The divorce was one of my ex-girlfriends who married a friend. She came to me for advice and, as a result, she kicked him out. He rapidly became my best friend... but I care more for my ex than for him. I was even happy when they got divorced. I still fancy my ex a lot. But, as they say: having a bad conscience requires having a conscience to begin with. You create your own life.

- "Angry Advisor", 29

Hell Rating:

I haven't told my parents that I'm going to Gambia to get married. I'm leaving on Monday and get married in Senegal on Saturday. I didn't tell them since I know that they would try to stop me. We've already had a major disagreement about this. So it will have to be a "normal wedding" when 'X' gets here. I also want to say that JH's been in jail for rape. And that I've been arrested for being drunk and disorderly, but I know that you have too, Mom. Hugs; I love both you and Dad anyway.

- Sera, 30

Hell Rating:

My neighbours let their dogs piss on my lawn, now I've put out rat poison to get back at them.

- "Pissed Off Poisoner"

Hell Rating:

I can't stand people who use "I" and "me" incorrectly. If someone writes "visit my sister and I" and thinks that he's clever for not writing "me" it upsets me for the rest of the day.

- Ellen, 27, Art director

Hell Rating:

When my mom turned 40, her friend gave her a large black dildo. Since she didn't want it, she threw it away. Some friends and I took it and wrapped in nice paper, attached a note saying "From your secret admirer" and put it in the mailbox of a boy in class we didn't like. A while later his parents divorced.

- Anna

Hell Rating:

I'm an employer. I like to be mean to my employees. I take great pleasure in catching someone making a mistake. I can dwell on it for months by referencing to it with little hints. If I get the opportunity to give someone a warning, it's a special occasion for me—particularly if the person starts to cry. I'm always looking for faults so that I can hassle my staff.

I love being an employer. Maybe I'm just bored?

- "Mad Manager", 47

Hell Rating:

When I was ten, I had a wish that Thomas Brolin would get injured on the football field so that I could come down to the field and save him. The very autumn I wished this. I was at the game between Sweden and Hungary— the one where Thomas broke his foot which lead to the beginning of the end of his career. I never went down to help him! Powerless, I sat on the stands watching my dream come true.
It's tough to carry something like that when you're only ten years old.

- Darren, Consultant

Hell Rating:

I killed a budgie. I was only six or seven years old and didn't know what I was doing. I thought that the bubbles coming out of his mouth looked funny. I panicked when he stopped moving. It took years before I realized that I had drowned him. I felt very bad for my poor bird.

I never meant for him to die. God, I'm sorry.

- Marilyn, Medical school

Hell Rating: 🔥🔥🔥🔥

Hi, God. Once, when a friend and I were swimming, we saw a squirrel up in a tree. It had some kind of naked little animal in its mouth. I thought it was a rat and started to throw pine cones at it. Eventually the squirrel screamed and dropped the naked animal. It came down the tree to look for it. I don't know if it found it, but later I understood that it must have been a baby squirrel in its mother's mouth. I hope it didn't die.

I'm so incredibly ashamed. Never ever hurt animals!

- "Secret Squirrel Killer", 22

Hell Rating:

I can't see what's so bad about paedophiles.
Personally, I'm not turned on by kids, but find people who eat shit way more disgusting. That ought to be illegal. I suppose I'd run into some problems if I were to vent my opinion more openly.

- Johnny, Bouncer

Hell Rating:

Hi, God-
When a friend and I were shopping, we spotted an old classmate of ours. He didn't recognize us, so we decided to put underwear with electronic tags on them in his pockets as revenge. When he left the store, the alarm went off and the police arrived. I don't think we've had this fun since we pushed the same friend down a flight of stairs when we were kids.

- Helen, 28, Shop assistant

Hell Rating:

Sometimes when my neighbours have left for work, I walk over to their front door and pee in their mail slot.

- "The Underground Urinator", 28

Hell Rating:

Once, when I spent the night at my boyfriend's place, I went through his stuff when he was on the toilet. What I found scared me, to say the least. In a drawer, I found 23 bags of dried faeces. You might ask yourself how I knew it was faeces. Partly because of the smell once I got one bag open, and partly because I later found little labels on them. They had dates and description of the poo on them, like one smelled like mint and another had colour like marble cake. Need I say that I dumped him shortly after this?

He's now a reality show celebrity and would die if this got out.

- Anonymous Poo-Ex

Hell Rating:

When I worked in a bank this summer, I got into all kinds of mischief with one of the girls working there. We'd steal this guy's pen and hide it - nonsense like that. Once, we put the pen on his chair so that he'd get it right in the ass when he sat down. When he did sit down, he got the pen on his caudal vertebra and was in a lot of pain because he had scoliosis. He never understood that we were to blame, but it still felt terrible. He had to go to the doctor because of this.

- Josephine, 27, Student

Hell Rating:

I lie on the internet, claiming to be bulimic.
I spend time on pro-anorexia/pro bulimia websites, chatting and mailing with lots of people with different eating disorders. I lie about how long I've been sick and I'm even on a fast with a girl living somewhere in the USA, but really I eat plenty every day.

- Anna, 23, Actress

Hell Rating:

I work as a 911-operator, meaning I take calls from people in distress. I'm also considered to be one of the best workers there. But I'm not. I hang up the phone if it gets too hard. I call the callers bitch, whore, queer, psycho and cunt when my colleagues can't hear. Furthermore, I make the confused psychos calling even more paranoid by feeding their delusions. I hate being responsible. All I want to do is smoke weed until I pass out, have sex with prostitutes, go to strip clubs, shoot people with an Uzi and perform planned bank robberies.

But I keep answering the phone and die.

- "The Enraged Emergency Operator", 35

Hell Rating:

I work at the local library and when no one is watching, I tear out pages from the books.

I don't know why.

- "Bookish Bystander", 42

Hell Rating: 🔥 🔥 🔥

My mom was a babysitter once and sometimes I had to help her watch the kids for different reasons. I'd lock kids in the bathroom and, man, did they cry. I'd keep them there for several minutes. I did this a lot.
I used to scare them by giving them the evil eye over breakfast.
When they cried, I pretended like I didn't know why.
This is not all I have on my conscience.

- Sebastian, 20, Unemployed

Hell Rating: 🔥 🔥 🔥

When I've had a fight with my parents, I take their toothbrushes and swirl them around in the toilet. Then I scrub them against the edge where the shit gathers. To hell with them sometimes.

But I love them so much!

- Carolyn, Student

Hell Rating:

When I was twelve, some friends and I burned an eight-year-old on the hand with a magnifying glass. It smelled of burnt flesh and he screamed. The trauma probably gave him psychological problems. The reason we burned him was that he threw sand at us. I'm now studying to become a social worker.

- Danny, 28, Student

Hell Rating: 🔥🔥🔥🔥

I fantasize about killing art directors and copywriters.

- "Art Director Adversary", 35

Hell Rating: 🔥🔥🔥

When my sister and I were little, we spent our time trying to "exterminate" all the stinging jellyfish we could find by catching them with a big net and then hack them to bits on land...

sorry, all jellyfishies...

- Rebecca, 26, Receptionist

Hell Rating: 🔥🔥🔥🔥

I often spit in the hamburgers I make at work.

- Mike, Chef

Hell Rating:

Whenever I ride in the same car as my mother-in-law, I want to strangle her. Slowly. The woman drives like an idiot, either recklessly or completely passively, and more often than not - both.
My urge to strangle her is particularly strong when she drives precisely 5 m.p.h. under the speed limit, something she tends to do (for whatever reason). Luckily, I'm not in the habit of carrying a gun. I really have to bite my tongue and clench my hands in my pockets as not to make my wife motherless.

- "Irate In-Law", 26

Hell Rating:

I do my dishes under running water. I never recycle – everything goes into the compost container. I poured half a gallon of diesel into the sink. In a nutshell, I don't give a damn about the world. I trust it'll stay in one piece until I'm dead and after that I don't give a fuck! Naturally, I still claim to be a friend of the environment and want to make my contribution to the cause just like everyone else.

- "Enraged Environmentalist", 28

Hell Rating:

I'm a booking agent for a major airline and sometimes I hang up on customers who are trying to book a flight.

- Anonymous, 39

Hell Rating:

I hate my co-workers and sometimes spread false rumors to start trouble - make people hate each other. They never know I'm to blame. Small words can create big conflicts.

- "Can't Bear Coworkers", 33

Hell Rating: 🔥🔥🔥

I worked as a waiter at a posh hotel a while back.
I really hated all the snobbish people who ate there.
I was constantly in a crappy mood, so I lightened my mood by doing certain disgusting things to their food before serving it.
Pissing off a waiter is probably one of the most stupid things you can do.

- Robin

Hell Rating: 🔥🔥🔥

My job is boring as hell. To brighten my days, I entertain myself by stealing and destroying things - items in the mail and property belonging to the Post Office. I sometimes don't bother delivering mail to the customers I hate. I also enjoy making work harder for my colleagues.

- Ron, 46, Mailman

Hell Rating:

I work at a law firm and I've deliberately lost several cases because of anger towards my clients.

- Eric, 46, Lawyer

Hell Rating:

I sometimes wish that my girlfriend's kids didn't exist!
I love them like they were my own, but sometimes you think like this.

- "Daddy Dearest", 42

Hell Rating: 🔥🔥🔥🔥

Once, after fighting with my boyfriend, I crushed three Viagra pills and put them in his food. He had to stay at home for quite a while.

- "Quicker Pecker Upper", 34

Hell Rating: 🔥🔥

I hate this guy I work with.
Sometimes I fantasize about running him over with my car.

- Jeremy, 28, Sales Rep

Hell Rating: 🔥🔥🔥

I´ve sent an anonymous email at the office, accusing our boss of some things, because I was pissed off. Now everyone is talking about it, wondering who it was.
I´m scared.

- Juanita, 26, Executive Secretary

Hell Rating: 🔥🔥

Always when I´m waiting for the bus I wonder what it would be like to push someone out in front of it. What would happen to my life.

- Susan, 32, Maid

Hell Rating:

Once, when I was out walking, it started to rain alot and all these frogs came out. We passed a golf course and we filled this golfball washing machine with frogs and turned it on. It was really gross.
Sorry frogs, you rock.

- Meredith, 24, student

Hell Rating: 🔥🔥🔥🔥

Sometimes I wish my girlfriend would die in some horrible way, so that I could be this exciting, mysterious person.

- George, 26, Stockbroker

Hell Rating:

Sometimes I fantasize about killing my wife to be able to do what I want, like move abroad or become an artist.

- Phil, 42, Insurance Adjuster

Hell Rating:

Babies have the smallest fingers, they look so fragile. Sometimes I imagige biting them, I mean really hard, almost breaking them. Off course I would never do it, but the thought of it is tempting.

- Lillian, 28, Nanny

Hell Rating:

Everytime I walk past someone really ugly or dirty person, I feel the need to hold my breath. I don´t want to but I feel I have to.

- Fabio, 29, Hairdresser

Hell Rating:

I fantasize about lighting myself on fire an running around like a big torch. Ever since I saw a picture from India about someone doing this, I´ve had problems letting go of this thought.

- Tom, 30, Police Officer

Hell Rating: 🔥🔥

I sometimes look for, and answer, sex ads on the 'net even though I'm living with my boyfriend and have children with him.

I've even answered with nude pics of myself.

- "Sex Surfer", 37, Store Manager.

Hell Rating: 🔥 🔥 🔥 🔥

I'm active in a youth association and I'm a proclaimed feminist.
I attend meetings about the oppression of women in all its forms,
porn being one of them.
But I can't resist my drive to watch hard core porn.
It always makes me feel very bad afterwards.
Imagine if people found out what I'm doing.

- "Anonymous Activist"

Hell Rating:

I'm a urologist and have, in my line of work, had my finger on many prostates.
This Monday, I had a patient whom I found very attractive.
I examined his prostate and found it to be swollen.
After he left the room,
I went and jerked off without taking off the gloves.

- "Passion for Prostrates", 40, Urologist

Hell Rating: 🔥 🔥

My girlfriend just caught me surfing some dating sites on the net.
I guess I'll be buying a lot of flowers and chocolates for a while.
I didn't tell her that I'm seeing a couple of the net-babes for sex every now and then.

- "Anonymous Amore"

Hell Rating: 🔥 🔥 🔥 🔥

When I was in Italy, I had sex with a woman who turned out to be a man.
I was so surprised that I just got up and left.

It was like something you see in a movie.

- "Anonymous Crying Game", 25

Hell Rating: 🔥

I've had sex with the calves at my farm.

- "Anonymous Animal Lover", 38

Hell Rating: 🔥 🔥 🔥 🔥 🔥

I try to masturbate in the most bizarre places I can think of. I have done a list of the places I've "done". On it I have, among other places, two big churches. I'm a Christian myself and work in a church.

- "Wandering Wanker", 37

Hell Rating:

When I'm alone in my apartment - I let my dog lick me.

- Lisa, 30

Hell Rating:

I'm over 40 years old and have been unfaithful many times. I look at young girls a lot. I'm tired of married life and so on and so forth. I think most "old men" can relate to my feelings.

- John, Self-employed

Hell Rating:

When I jerk off, I like to fantasize about biting the heads of goats and small birds. I then continue the sex (in my mind) with the left over carcasses.

- "Wild Animal Love", 46

Hell Rating:

I peep through my 15-year-old neighbour's window when she changes her clothes. I'm not sure if she's seen me.

I'm thinking of taking pictures of her.

- Michael, Self-employed

Hell Rating: 🔥🔥🔥🔥

I have on two separate occasions stolen G-strings, belonging to unknown girls, from the laundry room.

- Mitchell, 61, Senior Citizen

Hell Rating: 🔥🔥🔥🔥🔥

I've called female classmates and jerked off while asking them trivial questions about our homework. But I don't do it anymore.

- "Handwork, Homework", 26

Hell Rating:

I lived with two girls in a dorm room a few years ago. One weekend, I got the idea to install a webcam in the shower. After that day, I videotaped them every time they took a shower or went to the loo.

- "Anonymous Pervert"

Hell Rating: 🔥🔥🔥🔥

Sometimes, when I talk to male executives in a meeting, I think "wonder what would happen if I kissed him?" This happens a lot, but I'd never act upon it. I sometimes think it about the female executives as well, but not as often.

- Craig, 25, Sales

Hell Rating:

I have an obsession with people with oddly-shaped (meaning slim) heads. When I come across people with this condition, I smile at them, listen to what they say and laugh at their jokes. All my mental capacity is spent fantasizing about the circumstances surrounding their birth, and their mother's crotch. Babies are born with soft heads, so I always think about how their skulls have been shaped by their mother's crotch when they were pushed out of her. I know it's a bit gross, but I can't stop thinking about it.

- Toby, 28, Student

Hell Rating:

I work as an electrician and have installed surveillance cameras in the fitting rooms of several large clothing stores. My friend is a security guard who works for most of the stores and he collects the tapes daily. It feels oddly exciting to see all the unsuspecting people get undressed.

- "Vivacious Videotaper", 33, Electrician

Hell Rating:

I cannot stop looking at breasts. As soon as I get the chance - it doesn't matter if it's a friend, stranger or classmate - I stare like crazy for as long as I dare. Don't know why really, but it's very nice.
With it being summer, which means fewer clothes,
it's party time for me.

- "Boob-lover", 23

Hell Rating:

First I fell madly in love with a girl... was too afraid to make contact, and later fell in love with another girl who became my girlfriend. The whole time I was still in love with the first girl. Shortly after, I messed around with a third girl. When I broke it off with my girlfriend—after several years—I got together with the first girl. Or, rather, we got together before I had the time to break off the other relationship. After two years, I dumped her and got together with the girl I hade messed around with years earlier. I then realized that I still had a crush on the first girl and so messed around with her. I love her!!! I don't think I give a damn about the others!! Does it sound complicated? Imagine if they found out about each other!!

- "Loyal Lover", 20

hell Rating:

My friend doesn't know that I'm the father of one of "his" children. He isn't suspicious and he takes really good care of the child.

- "Secret Daddy", 37

Hell Rating: 🔥🔥🔥🔥🔥

I've always been kind of racist, but lately I've been dreaming of getting a large black dick up my ass. I'm not gay, but I still want to know what it feels like. I don't know what to do.

- "Randy Racist", 31

Hell Rating: 🔥🔥🔥🔥🔥

I'm secretly a transvestite and get off on wearing women's clothing. The more formal the outfit, the more turned on I get. I've ordered several wedding dresses online. When they get here I'll put on panties, bra, pantyhose, gloves, underskirt, dress – everything – and lie on my bed and jerk off. I'm also turned on by wearing diapers.

- "Pre-Op Postal Worker", 29

Hell Rating:

I live in my boss's house, and even though I'm single, I feel bad about being attracted to her. I smell her panties and stuff, but only when I'm 100% sure that she doesn't know. I feel really bad about this, partly because she's more then twice my age.

I don't know what to do with myself.

- John, Waiter

Hell Rating:

My ex-girlfriend used to work part time in a church. One night, when I picked her up, we sneaked into the cathedral and had sex on the altar.

- "Coital Catholic", 26

Hell Rating:

When I was little, 5 or 7 years old, I was very curious about the human body. I asked a girl I knew to show me her butt, just because I wanted to see what it looked like. I also asked a boy I knew to show me his turd. I'm a boy myself and have NO IDEA why I even asked him to do this. We also had a club where we touched each other's willies and even sucked them. Once my friend crapped on my other friends willie. I'll have to live with this for the rest of my life and it's killing me. If it came out I would undoubtedly kill myself.

- "Butt-loving Actor", 30

Hell Rating:

Last week we had a cosy evening at a friend's place. Chips and movies on the menu. I was in charge of the dip. When I stood there all alone in the kitchen, I got this overwhelming urge to put my dick in the dip. Eventually I stood there with garlic dip all over my thing. It was fun, and even more so when my female friends ate the dip.

I can still laugh myself to sleep thinking of it.

- "Oral Electrician", 35

Hell Rating:

I'm a very normal girl who's afraid of dogs. The thing is that I sometimes fantasize about having sex with someone in front of a big dog. I've also fantasized about the dog a few times.

God, forgive me...

- Anna, 24, Student

Hell Rating:

The guy who likes me thinks that we're a couple, he wants me to move in with him (which I probably will, but only because it's more practical), but I tell people that I'm single since I don't want to get serious with him. At the moment, I'm into another guy and I've also had sex with his friend. Several times.

- "Expert in Exploitation", 25

Hell Rating:

I have on several occasions jerked off in my car.
Ought to add that this occurred while I was driving.

- "Autoerotic Automobile-lover", 32

Hell Rating:

I'm obsessed with masturbating at work. I go to the men's room every
coffee break and do it and leave my cum in the liquid soap dispenser.
So far, no one has noticed. It mixes with the soap, you see.
I just can't stop.

- "Wanker Banker", 40

Hell Rating:

When I had sex with my ex I used to fantasize about Pamela Anderson. It made me cum right away.

- "Anonymous Fantasizer", 42

Hell Rating: 🔥

I have a crush on my university professor. I love my boyfriend, but lately all I can think about is my professor putting me over his lap and spanking me.

- "Secret Spank-lover", 20

Hell Rating: 🔥 🔥

My ex and I had sex in a church.

- Gloria, 38, Journalist

Hell Rating:

I like to download gay porn. I don't really think I'm gay, I just like to look at muscular male bodies with hard dicks.

- "Dick Lover in Denial", 38

Hell Rating:

I have sex with a married woman at work every time I'm on call.
I'm married too.
I don't really like her, but it makes time go by a little faster.

- "Drowsy Doctor", 37

Hell Rating:

When I was about nine, my friend and I got naked and pressed Ken dolls (Barbie's boyfriend) against our bodies. We washed them later, luckily! I'm ashamed to confess it, I can't believe I did it.

- Tess, 30, Stylist

Hell Rating:

I like to watch or hear other people have sex.

- Maggie, Business Administration

Hell Rating:

I had sex with my mother-in-law last Saturday. My wife doesn't know, and I feel bad about what we did.
I deserve to burn in hell.

- "Lovers In-Law". 45

Hell Rating:

I'm a bus driver. In my line of work, you meet a lot of different people and many of them teens. It's common knowledge that teens and zits go together. But I suffer from an obsession: every time I see a zit, I get an urge to squeeze it! I'm ashamed of myself. When this urge comes over me, I let the teens ride for free.

- Steve, 39, Bus driver

Hell Rating: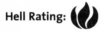

I´ve been together with my girlfriend for years, but I´m not happy with her. So I started to live a double life and I have another relationship with another woman on a different continent. I´m not really happy with her, either, but am afraid of being lonely. This is starting to be a big burden for me - not to mention the constant lying to both my "girls".

- Peter, Pilot, 38

Hell Rating:

I get sexually arroused when I watch horror movies. Mostly from the scenes where the murderer or monster chases the girl. I wouldn´t want to be chased myself, but it turnes me on by seeing it. Maybe I´m crazy. My boyfriend is begging to catch on to me, buy I don´t think he´ll say anything. He must think I´m a total pervert.

- Erika, 25, Dental Assistant

Hell Rating:

At night I sit in my bedroom and watch the girl next door take her clothes off. I´ve just got a pair of binoculars so I can see her even better now. She usually walks around in just her underwear.

- Paul, 36, Journalist

Hell Rating:

I had sex with my old teacher last weekend. She´s 26 years older than me, but she still looks good. The worse part is that I want to do it again.

- Richard, 25, Student

Hell Rating:

When I´m in a really boring meeting I sit and touch my willie through a whole in my pocket. I touch my bellybutton alot too, and in my nose. I put booggers under the table and I wonder if all the others do the same or what they would think of me if they knew. I mean I´m 45 years old but acting like a kid.

- Steve, 35, Corporate Executive

Hell Rating:

When I was younger I tried to get a baby cow to give me oral pleasure.

- Samantha, Farmer's Wife, 35

Hell Rating:

When I´m the last one left in our office I get down on my knees and sniff the chair where my very sexy college has been sitting.

- Charles, 30, Financial Advisor

Hell Rating:

I feel my girlfriend up when she´s sleeping.

- Robert, 36

Hell Rating: 🔥

When I´m at a girl's place (friend or girlfriend), I always try to steal a pair of used underwear from their dirty laundry. Now I have at least thirty pairs hidden and I´m terrified that my girlfriend will find them. Buy I don´t smell them or anything; it´s not like I´m a freak.

- Bill, 30, Doctor

Hell Rating: 🔥🔥🔥

I have this urge to smack a nice ass when it walks by. I wish girls would think it was the best thing ever to get their ass smacked.

- Rick, 35, Elementary School Janitor

Hell Rating: 🔥🔥🔥

These last few years I have special fantasies about girls. Every girl I meet, I wonder what it would be like having her accross my knee and spanking her bare bottom.
I pray to God people can´t see inside my head.

- George, 65, Retiree

Hell Rating: 🔥🔥🔥

I get really turned on by rubbing myself against other peoples furniture and entertainment systems.

- Marla, 32, Furniture Sales

Hell Rating: 🔥🔥🔥

I can't help masturbating in the shower. I´ll do it wherever I am - at a friend's house, at the gym, wherever it is I shower. I don´t know why. I guess it´s some sort of weird fetish.

- "Jerry", Swim Instructor, 32

Hell Rating: 🔥🔥

I have a problem. I love to wear diapers. There´s just nothing better. The best is when you actually "go" in the diaper, and it feels all warm and cozy. That feeling is unbeatable. I dare not tell anybody about this since I don't know how they would react. If you would like to try, however, but without actually "going", you could still experience the nice feeling if you use warm water, white flour and freshly boiled pasta. Mix it together to get the right consistency and put it in the diapers. Feels truly wonderful. I really want to tell about this because I dont want people with the same "problem" to feel that they are alone.

- Jimmy, 27, Gym Instructor

Hell Rating:

Gross-out Rating:

multiple

offenders

I sometimes forget to clean the cat's litter box. I'm also sulky towards my husband. I have too little contact with my friends. and I don't work as hard as I should on school. I stole while working as a floorwalker. I must have stolen at least $1000 worth of merchandise. All the while working to catch shoplifters.
No one suspected me; I was just doing my job.

- Susie, 42
Sins:Sloth, Greed

Hell Rating: 🔥🔥🔥

I read my ex's e-mail every day. I know the password from when we were dating. Kind of fun. He's got a new girlfriend and I read their private mail!
I guess I'm a bit bad after all.

- Maria, 25, Hotel receptionist
Sins: Envy, Wrath

Hell Rating:

Here we go:
I lie to everyone.
I'm dating a girl that I'm not one bit attracted to,
but she's kind and good in bed.
I jerk off in the company bathroom every day.
I do drugs at least ten times a month.
I brag.
I owe the government money.
I've also peed on the heating unit in the sauna at our gym.

- "Loopy Lister", 22
Sins:Pride, Lust, Sloth

Hell Rating: 🔥🔥🔥🔥

My best friends think I'm a considerate saint but they know nothing about what I'm really like. I smoke cannabis bought with money I steal from the big charity organisation I work for.

- "Secret Smoker", 34
Sins:Sloth, Gluttony, Greed

Hell Rating: 🔥🔥🔥🔥🔥

I managed to get early retirement and I'm pleased.
It won't make me rich, but at least I don't have to work.
Now I sell bootleg liquor to get some extra cash.

- "Aging Alcohol Seller", 46, Senior citizen
Sins:Sloth, Greed

Hell Rating: 🔥🔥🔥

A few months ago, my family got a bill from a porn site on the internet. I was the only one home that night, but I've maintained that I wasn't online at the time. But I was totally surfing for porn. The bill was for $80, but my dad won't pay seeing as "she would never do that".

- "Secret Sex Surfer", 19
Sins:Lust, Gluttony, Greed

Hell Rating: 🔥🔥🔥

I was once a bus driver and used to smoke two or three joints before going on my shift. Once a female passenger picked me up (I'm a 27-year-old guy) and we had sex in the back of the bus, when I was supposed to be picking up passengers. Whenever people paid too much, I kept the money myself. One freezing day I peed in the bus. It was like I owned that bus.

- Louis 27
Sins:Sloth, Lust, Greed

Hell Rating:

Hi. I broke my brother's headphones, but not on purpose. I pray to God even though I don't believe in God. I change tampons once a day on average. I stole a pack of cigarettes from my dad when I was thirteen. My girlfriend and I fingered each other in the tub at the same age. I've shoplifted a lot. I dumped my boyfriend because I had met someone else, but I didn't tell him that. I go through my family's secret stuff. Sometimes I eat my own snot. Once when I was little (eleven maybe) I took my younger relative's hand and put it on my genitals. I once crapped myself on the way home from a party. I stripped for two guys when I was ten. Bye.

- "Shadowy Sister", 22
Sins:Sloth, Greed, Lust

Hell Rating:

I once took a handbag off the floor in a club, went to the bathroom and looted it.

I've made fake doctor's notes to give to my boss. I hate her.

I do sloppy work.

I sometimes masturbate under the covers when my boyfriend lies next to me. He doesn't notice.

I've read my boyfriend's private notes.

I lie about how long I've been a vegetarian.

I lie about myself to make me seem more interesting.

In reality, I'm ugly but I get up early every morning and make myself really pretty.

I've skipped several classes in school but tell people that I've attended them.

- Drew, 25, Student
Sins:Sloth, Greed, Lust, Pride

Hell Rating:

I lied today.
I lied both to my mom and my husband.
I told them that I'm going to Holland on business.
In reality, I'm going there to do drugs and sleep around.
The worst part is that I'm not feeling bad about this at all, quite the opposite.

- "Ambitious in Amsterdam"
Sins:Pride, Lust, Gluttony

Hell Rating:

When I borrow money from people, I never have any intention of paying them back.
I behaved like a sadist once when I was young.
I found an abandoned bird's nest, or so I thought!!!
I filled it with firecrackers and lit them.
The baby birds were blown to bits.
I'm a bad person.

- "Mysterious Multiple Sinner", 25
Sins:Greed, Wrath

Hell Rating: 🔥 🔥 🔥 🔥

BLA BLA - 600 Incredibly Useless Facts
Something to Talk About When You Have Nothing else to Say
91-974882-1-6
Humor
March 2005

A Know-It-All's Handbook

Everyone needs something to blurt out during uncomfortable silences and
ice-breaker moments. This fascinating handbook of hilarious, arcane and
bizarre tidbits will make its bearer a hit at party conversation and trivia contests.

Dirty MovieQuoteBook
91-974396-9-X
Humor/Film
May 2005

Saucy Sayings of Cinema

With over 700 saucy, sexy quotes from the funniest and most sordid films
ever produced. A movie quiz game in a book. An excellent source of fresh
pick-up or put-down lines, this titillating guide is sure to put anyone in the
mood for love.

Cult MovieQuoteBook
91-974396-3-0
Humor/Film
May 2005

A Film Buff's Dictionary of Classic Lines

Over 700 memorable, provocative, hilarious and thought- provoking quotes fill this fascinating guide, a kind of dictionary for movie quote buffs. Going beyond the old standards such as "Here's Looking at You Kid," this handbook pulls quotes from a surprisingly eclectic variety of global cinematic gems, and will have even the most diehard movie buffs frantic to place the line with the film.

The World's Coolest Baby Names
91-974883-1-3
Pop Culture
July 2005

A Name Book for the 21st Century Parent

A perfect name guide to spice up any baby shower name game.
Baby names aren't handed down anymore, and the coolest names are as much from pop culture as from the Bible. Hybrid names from popular and arcane sources in literature, television, and film create some very memorable name combinations. Includes the amusing trivia behind the names' origins and is sure to spark scads of arguments in expectant families everywhere!

Gordon Gecko - Wallstreet - Kissy Suzuki - you only live twice -
Bobby Peru - wild at heart - Holly Golightly - breakfast at tiffany's -
Alexander de Large - a clock work orange - Phoebe Buffay - friends

The Pet Cookbook
Have your best friend for dinner
91-974883-4-8
Humor/Cooking
July 2005

Domesticated Delicacies from Around the World

On a global scale, one man's pet is another man's supper, and this wild cookbook shares the best recipes from around the world on how to prepare those delectable little dishes from the domesticated animal kingdom. Scorpion Soup with a Sting, Pony 'n' Pepperoni Pizza, Parrot Piroge, and Goldfish Tortilla Wrap are just a few samples of the eclectic world cuisine within. Decidedly not for vegetarians.

*No animals were hurt during the making of this book.

    SCORPION SOUP WITH A STING
    CREAMY PARAKEET PASTA
    PARROT PIROGE
    GUINEA PIG PIE
    GOLDFISH TORTILLA WRAP
    MUD TURTLE RISOTTO